AWESOME ATHLETES

TONY HAWK

Julie Murray

ABDO Publishing Company

visit us at
www.abdopub.com

Published by ABDO Publishing Company, 4940 Viking Drive, Edina, Minnesota 55435.
Copyright © 2004 by Abdo Consulting Group, Inc. International copyrights reserved in all
countries. No part of this book may be reproduced in any form without written permission from
the publisher.

Printed in the United States.

Cover Photo: Getty Images
Interior Photos: Corbis p. 5; Getty Images pp. 7, 8, 9, 14, 15, 17, 19, 21, 23, 24, 25, 29; *Sports
Illustrated* pp. 11, 13, 27

Editors: Tamara L. Britton and Jessica A. Klein
Art Direction: Jessica A. Klein

Library of Congress Cataloging-in-Publication Data

Murray, Julie, 1969-
   Tony Hawk / Julie Murray.
      p. cm. -- (Awesome athletes)
   Includes index.
   Contents: Tony Hawk -- Growing up -- Discovering skateboarding -- A newfound love --
Turning pro -- The making of an awesome athlete -- A fall from the top -- Back to the top --
Completing the 900 -- Tony Hawk today.
   ISBN 1-59197-489-5
   1. Hawk, Tony--Juvenile literature. 2. Skateboarders--United States--Biography--Juvenile
literature. [1. Hawk, Tony. 2. Skateboarders.] I. Title. II. Series.

GV859.813.H39M87 2003
796.22'092--dc21
   [B]   2003051839

Contents

Tony Hawk

Tony Hawk is one of the most respected names in skateboarding. He has invented more than 80 tricks that have put him at the top of the world rankings. Tony's 900 at the 1999 X-Games was one of the greatest moves in skateboarding history. No one else has ever been able to complete the 900.

Tony went from a tall, thin California kid to a world-renowned skateboarding **phenomenon**. He became a **professional** skateboarder at the age of 14 and **retired** from competition when he was 31 years old. Today, Tony does skateboarding tours, has his own clothing line, and owns a skateboarding company. His *Tony Hawk's Pro Skater* video games are top sellers month after month.

Tony has put skateboarding on the map. He has won more competitions than any other skateboarder. His moves on the **half-pipe** have awed people all over the world. Thanks to Tony Hawk, skateboarding is a growing sport that continues to gain recognition every year.

Opposite page: While Tony's tricks may look effortless, they involve many years of intense practice.

Growing Up

Tony Hawk was born on May 12, 1968, in San Diego, California. His father, Frank, was a salesman. His mother, Nancy, had returned to college to finish her degree. Tony was Nancy and Frank's fourth child. His **siblings** were much older than he was. His two sisters, Lenore and Patricia, were already grown and had left home when Tony was born. His brother, Steve, was 12 years older than he was.

Tony was a wild child with lots of energy. He kept his parents busy! "Instead of the terrible twos, I was the terrible youth," Tony has said. Tony was always in trouble at school and at home. He didn't know how or where to funnel all his energy. Tony's parents decided to have Tony tested by a **psychologist**. They found out that Tony had a very high **IQ** and was not being challenged enough in school.

Tony's parents introduced him to sports, hoping that they would help him channel his extra energy. Tony liked playing basketball and baseball, but he did not like organized sports. He was too impatient to sit around and wait his turn. He also didn't like the constant drills and practice time. He just wanted to get out there and play.

Tony hangs in the air while competing at the 1997 X-Games.

Discovering Skateboarding

When Tony was nine years old, Steve brought a skateboard home. He encouraged Tony to get on and try it out. Tony was able to ride the skateboard a short distance before the board slipped out from under him and

he fell backward. That was all it took. Tony fell in love with skateboarding and was hooked.

Skateboarding was challenging for Tony. It took a lot of practice and concentration. But, he loved the feeling he had and the sense of freedom he felt when he was skateboarding. And, he

Tony flies during the vert competition at the 2001 X-Games.

didn't have to wait around for anyone else like he did in other sports. Tony enjoyed the fact that with skateboarding, his success was up to him and no one else. Finally, Tony had found an outlet for all his extra energy. Soon, skateboarding was on Tony's mind all the time.

Tony got his own skateboard and spent most of his time practicing. His parents were very supportive of his new interest. They were glad that he had found something to keep him focused and out of trouble.

Tony pulls up out of the half-pipe at the 2000 X-Games in San Francisco, California.

A Newfound Love

One day in fifth grade, Tony went to a skatepark called Oasis. That day changed Tony's life forever. He saw other skaters performing tricks up and down the park's walls. Tony felt like he finally fit in somewhere. The kids that were at the skatepark were just like him.

Tony spent countless hours at Oasis. He wanted to be there all the time and constantly begged his dad for a ride to the park. Tony even took a job delivering newspapers to pay for his park pass. He loved skating at Oasis so much that his parents had to drag him home in the evenings. Tony became so involved with skateboarding that he quit playing basketball and baseball. He wanted to focus all his attention on skateboarding.

Tony's dad started the California Amateur Skateboard League, known as CASL. This organization set rules for skateboarding competition. Skateboarders competed for higher scores by performing their tricks. Tony did well in the competitions, and by age 12 he was one of the

best skateboarders in California. Tony was so good that a skateboarding company called Dogtown started to **sponsor** him in the competitions.

Tony began adding new twists or flips to existing moves. People took notice and tried some of his new tricks, such as the Ollie 540, the Kickflip McTwist, and the Varial 540. Tony was inventing new moves all the time.

Tony has invented several versions of the handplant, including the gymnast plant and the 1/2 elquerial.

Turning Pro

When Tony was 13, he received a **sponsorship** deal from a skateboarding company called Powell and Peralta. He became the youngest member of a team of skaters called the "Bones Brigade." They dominated skateboarding competitions.

In 1982, a few days after his fourteenth birthday, Tony turned **pro**. He was at a contest in Whittier, California. The registration form had two boxes, "pro" and "amateur." Tony decided he was ready to be a professional skateboarder, so he checked that box.

In 1983, Tony's dad created another skateboarding organization called the National Skateboarding Association, or NSA. This organization was the first professional skateboarding circuit. Tony joined the circuit and started winning competitions.

At the time, there was really no money in skateboarding. Winners usually won a few hundred dollars and some skateboarding equipment. But as the sport became more popular, prize money increased. Tony was also improving his form and competition style.

He won most NSA competitions and started making more money. Soon, Tony was one of the best skateboarders in the world.

Around this time, Tony's family moved to Cardiff, California. His new home was close to a skatepark called Del Mar Skate Ranch. This became Tony's new hangout and the place where many of his signature moves were created.

In 1986, Powell and Peralta designed a Tony Hawk signature skateboard. The company sold more than 20,000 of them. Tony also appeared in a skateboarding film, *The Search for Animal Chin*, which introduced skating on the **half-pipe** to many people. Tony's **vert** skating soon became a popular form of competition.

Eighteen-year-old Tony performs a flying kick-leap at Del Mar Skate Ranch.

THE MAKING OF AN AWESOME ATHLETE

Tony is one of the best skateboarders in the world.

1968	1981	1982	1992
Born May 12 in San Diego, California	Becomes youngest member of the Bones Brigade at age 13	Turns pro at age 14 at a contest in Whittier, California	Starts own company, Birdhouse Projects, with Per Welinder

How Awesome Is He?

Tony has won more X-Games medals than any other skateboarder. See how he compares to other amazing skaters.

Skater	Years Pro	Medals Won
Bob Burnquist	14	7
Pierre-Luc Gagnon	11	4
Rune Glifberg	13	5
Tony Hawk	**17**	**14**
Bucky Lasek	14	6
Andy Macdonald	9	12

TONY HAWK

DECKS: BIRDHOUSE
TRUCKS: FURY
WHEELS: BIRDHOUSE
HEIGHT: 6 FEET, 3 INCHES
WEIGHT: 170 POUNDS

1995

Wins the vert contest in the first ever Extreme Games

1999

Becomes the first person to ever land the 900; Retires at age 31

2002

Creates Boom Boom HuckJam, an action sports arena tour

2003

Wins Nickelodeon's Kids' Choice Award for Best Male Athlete of the Year

 Placed first in 75 percent of pro contests entered.

 First overall in the NSA Series from 1983 to 1993.

 Invented more than 80 tricks, including the 900.

 First recipient of ESPN's Action Sports Achievement Award in 2001.

Highlights

A Fall from the Top

Tony's life was changing quickly. When he was 17 years old and still in high school, Tony made more than $70,000. He was appearing in television ads and movies. He bought a house in Carlsbad, California, and lived there with some of his friends. He also met a woman named Cindy. They bought a second home together in Fallbrook, California, in 1988. In April 1990, Tony and Cindy were married.

Meanwhile, Tony had been traveling all around the world. Sometimes he would win $10,000 in just one competition. But a new form of skateboarding called street skating was gaining popularity. People were skating on railings and stairs in public places. By the late 1980s, **vert** skating was on its way out and street skating was taking over.

Tony was fast becoming a has-been in the skateboarding world. Money that Tony once won easily in competition was quickly disappearing. To help pay the bills, Tony's wife went to work as a manicurist.

Opposite page: Tony rides the half-pipe during the 2000 Tony Hawk Skate Tour.

Times were tough, and Tony barely had enough money to get a bite to eat.

In early 1992, Tony and his friend Per Welinder decided to start a skateboard company. They called it Birdhouse Projects. In December, Cindy gave birth to a son. They named him Hudson Riley.

But Birdhouse was losing money, so in 1993 Tony sold his house in Fallbrook to make ends meet. He decided to do a summer tour to promote his company. Since Birdhouse was broke, he had to haul all of the skaters and their equipment around in his own minivan.

But skateboarding was no longer very popular. Few people showed up at the **demos**, and Birdhouse didn't get paid for many of them. By the end of the tour, Birdhouse was even further in debt.

The next couple of years were even harder. In 1994, Tony and Cindy divorced. Then to make matters worse, Tony's dad was diagnosed with lung cancer. They knew Frank wouldn't live much longer.

Opposite page: Tony flips in midair.

Back to the Top

Despite tough times, Tony kept at it. He entered as many competitions as he could. And, he and Welinder continued to find ways to make Birdhouse work. After a while, Birdhouse finally started to make money. Even better, it became a respected skateboarding company.

Tony was still inventing new moves, but there was one trick no one had ever been able to complete—the 900. The 900 is two and one-half flips off the **half-pipe**. Many considered this to be the ultimate trick, but no one could do it. Tony had been trying to do the 900 for more than 10 years. He had broken his ribs and cut up his legs in those attempts.

In 1995, ESPN decided to host the Extreme Games, later called the X-Games. These games televised competitions in extreme sports such as skateboarding, in-line skating, and BMX biking. This was a big breakthrough in skateboarding. People all around the world would be able to watch skateboarding

Tony has won 14 X-Games medals with his awesome moves.

competitions on television. Tony and others hoped the X-Games would revive **vert** skating.

The X-Games were successful, and more than 700,000 people tuned in. Tony won the vert competition and finished second in the street competition. He was once again known as the best skateboarder in the world. The X-Games had a huge impact on vert skating. Like Tony had hoped, people were once again interested in skating on the **half-pipe**.

Unfortunately, Tony's dad died shortly after the games. Despite this, Tony's personal life began to get back on track. In 1996 he married Erin, who had been a **professional** in-line skater. They moved into a brand new house. On March 26, 1999, Erin gave birth to a son, whom they named Spencer.

Tony continued to enter competitions and perform well. He also started a clothing company called Hawk Clothing. He became a household name throughout the world. Tony Hawk was back on top.

Opposite page (from L to R):
Tony, Spencer, Erin, and Riley

Completing the 900

At the 1999 X-Games in San Francisco, California, Tony became the first person to ever complete the 900. Tony was competing with four other skaters in the "best trick" competition. All the skaters had 30 minutes to show their best stuff to the crowd.

As the time was running out, people realized that Tony was attempting to perform a 900. The crowd cheered him on, and the other skaters moved away to give Tony the space he needed. Tony tried again and again to land the 900. He would come close, but he could not complete the trick during the allotted 30 minutes.

When time ran out, the crowd continued to chant,

Tony competes with Andy Macdonald in the vert doubles at the X-Games.

It took Tony 10 years and countless tries to successfully land the 900.

"Nine hundred! Nine hundred!" Tony continued skating, trying to complete the 900. On his eleventh try up the **half-pipe**, Tony completed the two and one-half flips in the air, but could he land it? He came down hard on his board and was able to keep his balance. Tony Hawk had finally completed the 900! "This is the best day of my life!" Tony yelled. The crowd erupted and skateboarding would never be the same.

Later that year, at 31 years old, Tony Hawk **retired** from skateboarding competition. He was almost 10 years older than most other competitors. He chose to quit while he was on top.

Tony Hawk Today

Tony Hawk is known around the world as the ultimate skateboarder. Even though he doesn't compete anymore, people still know he's the best skateboarder of our time.

Tony and Erin had another son, Keegan. He was born July 18, 2001. Tony lives in Carlsbad, California, with his wife and sons.

In 2002, Tony created an action sports arena tour called Boom Boom HuckJam. This tour is a **choreographed** action sports show that displays top athletes from **vert** skating, BMX stunt, and freestyle motocross. Live punk bands play at the shows. The tour was a huge success that year, and more than 10,000 people attended some of the 24 shows across the United States.

Tony has become a role model for many children around the world. His ability to relate to them and his willingness to share the sport of skateboarding has made him quite popular. This was evident at Nickelodeon's 2003 Kids' Choice Awards. Tony beat out

Tony chills outside his Carlsbad home with (from L to R) Spencer, Riley, Keegan, and Erin.

Kobe Bryant, Shaquille O'Neal, and Tiger Woods to win the Best Male Athlete of the Year award.

Tony's company, Birdhouse Projects, still tours around the world giving skating **demos**. They continue to produce top-of-the-line skateboards and market a Tony Hawk clothing line. Tony also had a hand in creating one of the top-selling video games, called *Tony Hawk's Pro Skater*. In 2003, *Electronic Gaming Monthly* named *Tony Hawk's Pro Skater 4* Action Sports Game of the Year. The fifth *Pro Skater* installment, *Tony Hawk's Underground*, is sure to be popular as well.

Tony has brought the sport of skateboarding to the top. Every day new skateparks are opening throughout the world. Tony created the Tony Hawk Foundation to further this cause. Each year he donates more than $400,000 to nonprofit groups that build skateparks in low-income areas of the United States.

Tony never dreamed that skateboarding would be his life. But, he is an example of how hard work and determination can help anyone make it to the top.

Opposite page: Tony attempts to jump into a tub of slime at the 2003 Kids' Choice Awards.

Glossary

choreograph - to plan a set of moves.

demo - a term that is short for the word *demonstration*. A demo shows examples of a product or activity.

half-pipe - a U-shaped ramp on which skaters do tricks.

IQ - a term that is short for *intelligence quotient*. This is a number used to show how smart someone is, based on his or her age group.

phenomenon - someone or something that is exceptional or unusual.

professional - working for money rather than pleasure. Sometimes, the word *professional* is shortened to *pro*.

psychologist - a person who specializes in studying the mind and the reasons for the way people think and act.

retire - to quit a professional career.

sibling - a brother or sister.

sponsor - a company that provides an athlete with money for wearing its clothing and using its equipment during competition.

vert - a term that is short for the word *vertical*. It can mean skating on ramps, pipes, or flat surfaces that angle up.

Web Sites

To learn more about Tony Hawk, visit ABDO Publishing Company on the World Wide Web at **www.abdopub.com**. Web sites about Tony Hawk are featured on our Book Links page. These links are routinely monitored and updated to provide the most current information available.

Index